Oldisms, Poetry
& Pandemic Prose

Becky Wallace

When you begin your read I want you to realize this isn't just about getting old or heartache. I wrote this hoping it would resonate with all. It's about growth and change, about good and bad. But most of all? It's the truth written from my heart. You will laugh, you will cry, and maybe, just maybe, make you think. I wear my heart on my sleeve but it's to be seen not ignored. Life is not all glory but learning to age with grace and dignity. Love life, live life, learn from life and age with living.

ISBN 978-1-7328169-4-7 (Paperback Edition)

Book design by Becky J. Wallace
Cover art by Becky J. Wallace
Published by Becky J. Wallace

BECKY WALLACE

OLDISMS

The once was.

Old age has become such a stigma that we are supposed to adhere to in life yet not all oldies are the same. When young we think we hold all the answers like in a card game that we don't have a clue what we are doing. All we can concentrate on is that pot in the middle of the table hoping we hold the right cards in our hands. Then when old age hits, which I personally hate being classified as old age person, we know how to hold the cards because we now have a full house. We know how to hold them and play them. Seniors can milk this to the fullest. Isn't it funny how we conveniently forget some things and remember a lot of other things that people think we should forget? I like this age even though it sucks at times yet I can embrace it at other times. I never knew I could play this card game so well. Embrace this old age to the fullest and just maybe you will feel a lot younger getting old.

Way Back When

Standing in the doorway,

the sun beating on my skin.

Reminds me of the sweeter times,

way back when.

People don't take time to open up

old doors,

they rush through life,

as if they are keeping score.

Memories come

and some may go,

that I know for sure.

So take some time,

sit back and smile

and open your old door.

Opinions of The Voice

We are born with a voice. We let everyone know we have arrived. Loud and clear we cry. Our families love to hear this because it means we have made it. Soon our sounds become so precious no one can hardly believe how sweet a sound can be. Those precious sounds become words that lead to sentences. How smart we are, how much we have learned from just our families? We soon start school and our voices are heard loud and clear. Our voices become opinions that don't necessarily agree with everyone else. Through the years as we grow we do listen to others and start understanding that we aren't always right and we can always learn from others. When we grow a little older and have children of our own it is our turn to hear that cry as they emerge and now we know how our parents felt.

Even then we continue to learn and only hope we do our children justice through the process of life. We raise them, hopefully, to be a good person with values like we were raised with. Let them know that they have a voice, a voice that can be heard and possibly change some things that possibly wouldn't have without that voice. Then we get old, our children are raised and we have done a good job. Sometimes better than we expected. We are so proud of the people they have become and the voices are now so precious to hear. We have missed them and want to know everything that they have been doing. Then one day we realize that getting old comes with drawbacks. That precious voice we were born with no longer is heard. Our opinions don't seem to be important like they used to be. Our cries are now just an echo in an empty room. Our cries are fading like the sunset to drift away with the winds of time.

Darkened Corner

How I love this darkened corner of my world. It takes me back to a time whereas a child we go there like when we made tents out of blankets and clubhouses under a tree limb throwing a sheet or blanket over it so this was our secret place. How special were those times when we used our minds to create these places? They call to me now, close your eyes and listen to the silence. How do we get there now? Darkness is so different as we age. I have lived there a lot in my life. No tree limbs or blankets to make my darkened place. Now I must go there to protect myself from the creature of adulthood. From this knowing disease of the mind becomes a sickness of the body we live in. At first, I was afraid of this place. Not like when I was a child I enjoyed my secret place, thinking I couldn't be seen by anyone.

As an adult when I go to my secret place it's different because I can still be seen and have to play a different game than when I was a child. I have to go there to keep my sanity and perform for others like an actress in a play. Can't let anyone know about this that I have lived with all my life and muster through so no one would know. Now as I age I still go there but now I can invite some to enter into my world because a whole lot of you are dealing with a form of my mind and body disease and it's not so hurtful as it used to be. Be sure I will not give up my darkened silent place but I can let others know I'm going there only because they understand what it's like on my stage of anxiety and the mental hell of my tale. Alas, I can complete my play of life as I've had to live it to applause and standing ovations for overcoming most of my illness. I'm now starting Act two and if anyone needs to know what it's like I will act on till the final curtain falls with the strength of mind and body that no one but me can perform.

When life throws
something bad your way.
Listen to what I have
to say...

...grab a bottle of wine,

you'll feel better

in wine time.

Be Still My Heart

Be still my heart, umm no don't be still cause that would mean I'm dead and speaking these words from my grave. A little humor there lol. Actually, I wish my words were heard among all generations. With that, I'm speaking to mostly these middle-aged and younger generations more than us seniors. I personally am getting more frustrated with every scroll of the phone to every newscast I see. No one talks about seniors. In this digital world, we are a lost part of society. No one ever thinks about asking us, how we are surviving in this tech world we live in. Myself? Not very well. I watch as these giants suppress smart and common sense people. This world no longer cares about simple things, they make everything political. Seniors are no longer an important part of this terrible world we live in. Manners and respect no longer apply and morals I have watched thrown out the window of time to take a slow drop to die from our vocabulary.

Oh, there are a few of us who still believe in the way we were raised. Right from wrong has become more who cares and the "I I I" and "me, me, me" forgetting about the way a person was raised. My heart hurts thinking how horrible it is to put so much stock into a scroll of a screen to tv trying to change the way we all think. I wish I could go back to a more loving way, instead of, will I be able to make it mentally, physically, and monthly with what little we seniors get that we worked so hard to obtain. I am so grateful for my sons who help me with this growing old. They try to help me understand this digital world we live in even though they too have a difficult time understanding it sometimes. I guess that makes me feel a little better. With all this said I choose to not give up and to try to keep my feelings the way I was raised to do. I will close my eyes and go back in time when it was the little things that I loved and miss every day. Politics were not the conversation around the dinner table or as a matter of fact, I don't remember them ever being talked about. Hummmm, food for thought?

Puzzle Pieces

Life is a puzzle we dump out every day looking for the right pieces, not knowing where to begin and wondering where the last piece will fit in, if ever. Every day more pieces appear to fit. Gosh, the life puzzle is hard to connect. When we start it there is so much to see. Oh, here's a piece so young, wow that was me.

We travel through time and fit our pieces to family, you know, some people's puzzles have a lot more pieces to fit. Yes, there are big pieces and some small, even tiny pieces that we can't believe we found and they fit perfectly. Then there are ugly pieces every puzzle has and they are so big it's easier to see them and fit them in. Sadness goes with them and we really wish they didn't fit at all. Guess what pieces I found that do fit? The joy pieces bring us happiness and definitely outweigh the sad ones because they fit perfectly in this life puzzle. Onward we go, struggling to finish this.

Oh dear, it's time to find the last old pieces. At first, some of them fit easily. Day after day we continue to fit more pieces thinking we will finish but there is a twist. One day you come in and think yours is done. It's not. We can never see it finished. The last piece belongs to someone else.

When we're gone, our loved ones can complete it for us. They will have to start their life's puzzle. It will be different for their eyes to see. Life's puzzles are really never truly done.

We can be watching from afar to guide them to find the right pieces which spell out LOVE. Life's puzzle is simply FAMILY.

Change?

Will things change? Will I change? My mind wants to make things different but my heart just isn't into it, or is it? I know I'm the captain of my ship but am I? Sometimes I think I'm floating away but where to? I crash upon the rocks of my ocean yet I'm still floating, am I? I know I can swim but feel like I'm drowning in my heart, can I swim? I'm holding my breath so I won't drown in my sorrow. Can I breathe?

My tears are still flowing, will they stop? I am so tired, yet, will I ever sleep? The nightmares are still there, are they really just dreams of a lost heart? Do I want the heartache to go, or should it stay? The answers are deep within me, are they? Am I afraid, yet, am I really strong? Do I still have a heart? I know it's there, or is it? Can things change? Can I change?

Shattered

My heart was broken when I was young by my first love. I picked up those hurtful pieces and put them back together. I was able to love again, I thought, after a few years my heart was broken again. This time the pieces were many and very difficult to put back. Took years, as if I was trying to put a very difficult puzzle together. All those pieces wouldn't fit for me so I put them back in a box and trudged on. Yes, it became a little easier with time and a few frogs along the way. So thankful I sent them to the lily pond of life before I croaked. All of a sudden the puzzle reappeared and I was able to put it together. Onward with life, I prevailed then a bombshell of emotions hit. Love again, how could this be? Very scary of the puzzle of broken pieces would return and it was hard to go there. Yes, I went full force and it was utter bliss.

Wow, what tornado hit me? I married for the second time, of course vowing I would never do it again. It was a good life for a long time, a very long time. Then boom my heart was not only broken but shattered into a million pieces. To this day I'm trying hard to put the pieces back but age has made that the toughest puzzle to fit back. When your young, all the time in the world you have. Even when your middle age you still have loads of time but when old not so much time is there. Ya know though that's ok because I guess you can have a complete puzzle of life. How, you ask, you learn that you don't need it all to fit. You learn to love yourself again. To be you that you probably lost along the way. I know I did, so now the puzzle of life is up on a shelf getting dustier day by day because it all doesn't need to fit.

Sitting here...

Sitting here aged and some would say old, feeling much like an old oak tree with branches floating out some with new growth yet some having died and need to be discarded. Some of my branches long for the way things used to be where new growth happens every year, some I would like to get rid of as quickly as possible because there's no growth, just brittle branches of time that will snap with a gentle wind to float blindly to the earth and will rot with time and become the dust that will blow away in the wind to become nothing. Then there's the new subtle growth, yes even-aged branches can have some new beginnings, even though there is so few that the sunlight makes a shadow that is small to none. My roots are waining and feel like it will not be long before a strong wind will take me down along with the old and new to be no more. While I can still feel the sun upon my time I will thrive and maybe one of the new growth on my branches will drop seed to the sweet earth below and root itself to begin another branch that will soak up the rain and flourish in the sun to always remind one that I was here and stayed strong for all that they may become apart of the forest of time.

Our emotions sometimes hide the truth.

Sometimes our truth hides our emotions.

Sadness is so like a disease that can overwhelm you in the blink of an eye, overtake your being as if you're living in a nightmare that never goes away. Fear of closing your eyes knowing the tears will forever come and soak your body as if you are burning up and can't escape it. Wishing you weren't you anymore, wanting to become another so you can live and not worry about the nights of tears that consume you. Maybe tomorrow all the tears will dry up and give you a day of being you, the you that made you, that belongs to another, maybe need you like before. With no more tears of the night to try to destroy you. Finding another to be the medicine of life to cure this tearful disease of sadness.

Mirror,

dear mirror,

on my bathroom wall,
tell me this is all?

The wrinkles,
you see,
are scary to me.

OH MY GOSH!

I have wrinkles on
my earlobes,
I see!

Where did these come from?

How much more is
there to be!

Aging

Where do I go, what do I do? Why is at my age there so much fear of the unknown? I want to do things and see things but it's almost as if I'm blind to what's around me. Call it what you will but to me, it is a handicap that I have lived with all my life. I see others venturing out on their own not a care in the world. Me, it's like I'm a child trying to walk but afraid to take a step. Am I the only older person like this? Who would know, because according to social media, no one is afraid to do or say anything? Maybe I'm the crazy one but surely others feel this way. Most people have a husband or wife to go with.

I have no one. I guess I'm just going to either sit here and wither away or kick myself and start traveling by myself. I truly hope that people know where I'm coming from. Living out here in the west is great but I have no friends and my kids well they work and I can't depend on them to entertain me for the rest of my life. I can see that this old baby needs to grow up and stop being so afraid of the unknown. Almost sounds like a mystery. To me, it is more than a mystery it's a novel of many tails to come and many trails to walk. People to meet and some to leave behind. Trying not to care but to always just be there, wherever that may be.

Happiness

Happiness, a word I'm not so sure of anymore. It seems to have a dark side I'm more familiar with. Oh don't get me wrong, most days I'm happy. More when I'm with my sons than anyone. It's just I through the years have depended on others to make me happy but looking back I guess in my first go around, I really wasn't. Probably only thought I loved him but naw! I didn't. The word thought says it all. The truly only happiness was having my kids. Even then there were times I'm sure weren't the greatest. Throughout our lives, we depend too much on others to make us better and supply our happiness. Really for me, I don't know. Again I fell in love with a great guy, younger than me but we were so happy. Gosh, the first few years were honeymoon after honeymoon.

Truthfully I was so foolish, thinking I was happy when all the time I was being used to fulfill both our happiness. The last years, there were a lot of things that happened to jerk us and me out of the enamor of my love. Slowly digging daily the death of love and burying the happiness. Then the funeral of our marriage was written and the final burial was upon me. The obituary was written which means the final resting place was in my mind and heart. Really and truly we all have had to bury our feelings at some time in our lives and carry sadness around hoping to lose it somewhere. Well, I have finally begun to find that I don't need another to bring back my happiness, I'm the only one who can master that book. The burial is complete and now I read my heart and mind with the truth of happiness.

Our minds can be the devil that stops us or the angel that keeps us going.

MY
BUTTERFLIES
HAVE
BECOME
TOO
OLD
TO
FLUTTER.

Back In Time

Daily my mind goes back in time, not too far but far enough where my vision is so clear, it doesn't need me to close my eyes over time even though I tend to anyway. It's a vision I will never forget and is with me every day. It makes me happy to see it and at times I feel like I have hugged it. It makes me stronger and realizes just how special it is to be able to embrace it. We laugh, we cry, and love so tight. I'm so thankful to get to enjoy it so much because of so many wonderful times we had together.

This vision was so smart and funny, loved by everyone it came in contact with. How I wish to this day for just a small moment to talk to it. Of course, I do talk to it every day but it is silent with just a smile of love. How can this be, this vision? We all have one that we can enjoy. Visions are for the living to help us go on. They never leave us just become silent to let us wander through our minds and enjoy them all over again. Best friends, buddies, partners, and the only true love you will ever know. I cherish her, my mom, and so glad to be able to call upon her vision and enjoy her as if she is here, silent, but forever.

Laying here my mind wandering as my eyes peer at the window of darkness seeing the moon and stars as they twinkle with life. So simple are they yet if we could get close to them they don't twinkle but change even in form. Life acts like the twinkle of the stars when we find our love our life shines like the stars and puts a glow on us like the moon. As the years go by the twinkle becomes nothing but light and the glow dulls with age. Staring now as I lay here wishing that twinkle and the glow was still a part of me, knowing it's not but even the love I had in my life has changed its form, no more to see that glow nor that twinkle because the shape of life has changed to a dull roar of emptiness, just left with a wish upon a star.

This depression is eating me alive,
like a lonely mind,
lost in the forest of never to be.
Trying to fight my way
through the alone darkness
hoping to see a glimmer of light
in the sea of thoughts
that I feel I will not see.
I am moving slowly,
wishing I had the energy
like I used to,
like I moved the mountains of life
and never flinched.
   Not so much anymore.
   Not so much anymore.
The need for me is not there.
As I wander through the trees of life
wishing I could cut them down
and see my horizon of strength
that was truly me,
knowing I will never be.
Will never be.

Chapters Close

I'm slowly starting to close another chapter of my being. I'm so tired of grieving this loss. Grief takes on so many different meanings in a person's life if you start thinking about it, it's not just from the death of a loved one. Throughout life, I have had a lot of different meanings of the word "grief", that it takes on a book of its own. I have grieved the loss of a lot of loved ones that I will never get over. I really don't believe I ever will. They are always in your heart and you manage to go on day by day. Then there's the child grief that's in all of us. First love grief, losing a pet, losing, etc, etc. I could go on forever with this list. The grief I'm referring to some will never go through and others may go through it once, others many times. I talking about the loss of a marriage. This one haunts you, hurts you, and takes time to get over it. I've been through this twice. First time I was shattered and took a long time for my heart and mind to heal.

The second time I'm still working through it but forgetting it better every day. It wasn't as shattering as the first but I'm a lot older so maybe I'm stronger. Yes, I am stronger, even though there are times I feel so weak and confused and just want answers as to why. To understand not to change anything but my thoughts. To have learned from this and to forget. I know in my heart I'll never have any answers, maybe this is what keeps the haunting of this loss. Putting my thoughts down in front of me to read is my doctor of the heart and mind. I've come to realize none of this is for me to understand but to build on and to create a better life for my heart and mind. I'm turning the corner of this page down hoping that I can close it sooner than later. They say time heals all but no, grief is always with us but it depends on the form as to whether that dogeared page once turned down will only be a marked page that turns to a blank sheet ready to live with these words.

Old Is My Excuse

I know we all have had it at some time in our lives yet I'm beginning to have a real hard time finding it or keeping it as a matter of fact. I'm learning the older I get that I don't need it as much anymore but I really should keep this around. If I lose it I'm afraid I'll lose me but if I keep it who will even see. It's hard to keep this up, so easy to let it go. There are days I have this and some days I'm too lazy to have it.

We all go through this, this I really don't care, yes this is hard to keep thought or actions to keep up. Oh being old does have dilemmas, maybe not as much as when we were young but I have my days where I really care about myself, then other days it's too hard to care. It sets me back for sure but I fight this caring, hoping I will bring it back. Maybe in the future, I'll find my care and be able to keep it again. If not oh well, old is my excuse for losing it.

I'm putting one foot in front of the other as if I'm on a mountain trail hoping I can climb up and forge forward as if I was a seasoned climber. Yet as I look up and see just how far I have to go I'll admit I don't know anymore if I have the strength to accomplish much more in my life. On this journey, I have ridden a roller coaster of life, many ups, and many downs but have learned to move forward with time. Forward is a hard word to accomplish the older I get. I know now that my life has always had the one thing I've been blessed with in order to continue this climb. Determination is a very large word with a very hard meaning but looking up I realize I haven't lost it, so I will keep putting one foot in front of the other until I set down on the peak of my life, and only then will I look back upon the horizon of my being and the sunset of my life.

We all should be living in the now
Some have lost just how.
Learn just how to play,
To make it thru the day.

Things have been hard for a while
Some have forgotten how to smile.
Worrying whose side they're on,
When we are all truly just their ponds.

Think twice about words you say,
You may hurt some, then you will pay.
Our written words won't go away,
Because of the times,
they are here to stay.

Speak only words from your heart,
be true with the words of your part.
Our words should not bring others to tears,
They should make you smile from ear to ear.

Stay kind in your loving way,
Learn again just how to play.
Think of all the ones you made smile,
You gave them that,
which will last a long while.

Pens

The terms of today forget about the pens of yesteryears, handwritten receipts even handwritten inventories. Dot here dots there my goodness the only dots I remember are when we finished a sentence. Oh yeah in case no one knows what I mean it was a period back when. Click on this, scroll up, scroll down, oh my never lookup. If you look up you might make eye contact which could be detrimental to your mind, or you might even have to speak, oh dear what to say. Digital this and that, our digitals were digits you know numbers.

Being an old-school person in this newfound world scares me. Why, because we as the old school generations may look up from these screens someday and there be a button to delete us. The irony of this, here I sit typing on a portable computer that knows what I'm going to type. Maybe this is better for the old because we forget sometimes what we were going to say. So embrace this computer life and the digital world so maybe just maybe they won't put that button to delete us beyond the digital grave.

We all go through life on a different path, only to end up at the same place.

Have you ever thought about the smile?
Making someone's day for awhile.
And what about a big hello,
Wishing ya didn't have to go.
Visiting someone who lives alone
Or calling them on the phone.
These are a few things we can do or say
To make a person feel good all day.
Don't take for granted while we are here
You will feel better spreading cheer.
So be thankful your here everyday
And smile, have a good day, you say!!!
It will make you feel good being this way!

Doorway of Life

Standing in the doorway of life I realize just how much life has changed. No longer are the ways I was brought up on exist in this foreign country I live in. I don't know if I'm living or existing anymore. I can only hope to see better days for us all. Will we ever truly experience any freedom that we have all taken for granted?

Remember when we would write with a pencil? When we said the pledge every day and pray? Walking to the store and buying popsicles and push-ups? Penny candy was the highlight of our journey? Not minding to walk everywhere or ride the bus? Having slumber parties or just hanging out under the street light? Riding bikes up the big hills and going so fast down them? Going to the pool and never getting in the water cause it wasn't cool?

Funny I could go on forever but there is so much life to think about. So much innocence and joy.

Stand in the doorway of your life and take a long journey back, those times were freedom! Those times were real life. Those times are ours, regardless, no one can experience it, dream about it or live it. This life belongs to me and to us. To never be lived again!

Prince Charming

How does it work? Obviously, I don't know because I have failed twice. With this said, I think about years ago when our parents married and started out. Most of them had nothing much to start with but they were happy. I'm sure times were tough for them all at times but they hung in there and grew together and stayed in love. Lived together, slept together, and worked toward a better life. What has happened to this kinda love? Oh, there are still a few of them but for the most part, people give up on each other. This world has made it too easy to dump one and have another before the ink dries on the papers. Lawyers get richer and people pay dearly not only in dollars but in pain and hurt from the loss. No one loves for long till they see another that maybe can afford them more, be it love, lust, or money.

They become strangers to each other and just go through the motions day by day until the ultimate explosion happens and they split. They find love on a phone, well they think they have but that's a lie too. People live in digital fairytales nowadays, because everyone's life looks so much better than theirs. Those endless years of love no longer exist. That's the fairytale. Most people are living a lie according to the phones. Remember Cinderella, that's what everyone's life looks like now but trust me that glass slipper doesn't fit, and at midnight that carriage will become a pumpkin and that Prince Charming you thought was there isn't anymore. Those things are not real life but loving and living are through a phone. Now whose really living a fairytale?

My generation was raised to respect...

new generation is raised to expect.

May It Rest In Peace

There is a sadness that has washed over me because I have to go to a funeral today for something I feel so much love for. I hope everyone attends one of these in their life, I know it sounds terrible that I would wish this upon anyone. I enter the house and look around at what's there. I see a kitchen table with loved ones sharing a meal with much laughter and fun. Oh, over there I see a mother and her children enjoying being outside, playing, huh? Then there is a son hugging his mother and crying because he's leaving the nest. Do you hear the church bell ringing, can't wait to go to Sunday school and church, all of us together? This is so hard for me as I see a daughter giving her mother a kiss on her cheek.

My tears are uncontrollable, why do I have to be here to see all this. As I gaze at all these memories realizing that nowadays so many of you have never experienced any of these treasured moments. Do you know why I'm attending this funeral? I'll tell you why people don't have this anymore in their lives. So many are too busy to see, to listen, and to enjoy the family as I knew growing up. It so saddens me that all people do is look down thinking they are seeing everyone's lives but the truth of the matter is they don't have a life. All they have is things. As I close the lid of this coffin of life, I can only hope that some will read this obituary and start being a family again. May it rest in peace.

The Old Times

As darkness wraps around your bed,
the stars light the visions in your head.
When times were simple and oh so sweet,
fairy's dancing at your feet.

Running barefoot in the field,
fighting the bad guys with a homemade shield.
Swinging from a vine to cross the creek,
hoping to land on your feet.

Cardboard sled on horse grass hills,
all we heard was lots of squeals.
Oh, let's do that one more time,
it hurt, but we lived, we were fine.

Freeze tag was our game of choice,
you couldn't quite your loud voice.
Everyone laughing and standing still,
til someone touched you, no more chill.

Hide and seek was such fun to do
better 'hide good' or they will find you.
Walking on gravel hurt your feet,
you didn't care, ya thought it was neat!

Sometimes go back in your dreams at night
hold onto those memories so very tight.
As the sun comes up to light your way,
sweet memories will make for a better day.

Reflection

The mirror on your wall is so much more than a reflection of you, it's the never-ending road map of your life. Look closely, you will find your roads, not interstates. We can behold our journey by looking at the wrinkles with age. Certain road wrinkles have a lot of meaning, around the eyes are the funny trip of your laughter. Bet you can remember a lot of those times. On your forehead, those roads are a worry. A lot of destruction is there with worry roads we can sometimes repair.

Oh my, the happy highway, looking and squinting to see or from the sunny days of happier times. Above the lips, we go this trip is from sipping from straws. Remember sharing that shake or maybe a sweet trip of kisses. Those wrinkle roads on your cheeks are the smile roads. Think back on the little things that you have forgotten were there in the roadsides in life. Need a vacation? Look beyond that mirror and you will see the best travel log and doesn't cost you a dime. Take some time for you to take this trip through your reflection in the mirror of time.

Looking at my hands
age is showing quite grand.
The wrinkles on my face
are in the right place.
My skin hangs everywhere,
no worries,
I don't care.
Eyes that once saw bright
can't go too far at night.
Ears that heard it all,
don't hear you when you call.
My way of walking fast
is something of the past.
Looking back I truly see,
aging will just be.
We all get old,
so I've been told.
That's ok with me.
I've lived, loved, and had a blast,
because of my young past.

You're never too old to start over again even
if it's with a friend. Travel in your dreams
where to be then open your eyes you will
see. It's not a dream that you're there, you
can go just anywhere. Take the time to look
around, your start is right there to be found.

Sometimes

I sit here sometimes and kinda glad I'm alone. That may sound funny but do you remember when you were young how when you were alone that you felt so big, almost like an adult. Walking in front of a mirror trying different hairstyles and dreamed of being all dressed up. Then your mom would yell, dinner is ready, but you weren't ready for it. Sighing, because you had to eat and leave your adult self behind for another time. I don't know about you but sometimes I wish I had someone to talk to or laugh with,

Instead of sitting here with the silence that becomes deafening and the tears start to flow down your face like a waterfall that sees no end. Looking for the life raft that will take you to a calmer place so you can regain yourself and hope you never feel that again, wanting to become that little girl again standing in front of the mirror playing adult once again. Hoping that sometimes to become the person you see in the reflection of the mirror of time all grown up and not playing but being.

Wandering

I find myself wandering aimlessly through the forest of memories in my mind. Like a starving creature digging through the thoughts of my life, not knowing what I will dig up. I never want to forget anything that I have buried deep into my being, be it good or bad.

I feed on my memories daily in hopes it strengthens me so I can keep wandering through to my heart and gain knowledge from some in hopes I don't make the same mistakes over and over again. I want to feel the goodness of love that I have felt before and miss so deeply now. I hope to someday fight my way through all the hurt and see nothing but joy like coming out of the forest to see the sweet sunrise and know I have another day to be a better person because of my mind and heart of memories from a time passed.

Poetry

My art of words.

When old you've lived life,
but that's when life should truly
be lived.

What a pleasant call I got yesterday,

My first true love made my day.

It's good to talk about our past,

Even though we didn't last.

A lot of life we both have lived,

Is it time for us now to give.

I'm not sure, only time will tell.

If we want to dip into that old well.

Regardless of the future that may be,

This is a true fairytale to me.

They lived happily ever after

Enjoying each other's laughter.

What I Found

I'm cleaning out the attic room,

I dread to see what I find.

But low and behold all the things were

Very, very kind.

I thought that I would blubber and cry the

whole way through.

I really didn't do that,

I'm glad that I'm not blue.

It took me back to fun times when

Everyone was here and let me hear the

laughter I hadn't heard in years.

These are my special memories that no

one can take away.

Cleaning out the attic just simply

Made my day.

Live.

In the moment.

Forever

Enjoy

Standing in the doorway.

Sun beating on my skin.

Reminds me of sweeter times,

Way back when.

People don't take time

to open up old doors.

They rush through life

as if they're keeping score.

Memories come and some may go,

that I know for sure.

So take some time, sit back, smile,

and open your old door.

I Am a Whisper

I am a whisper floating through air.

Someone is calling me out there.

Can you hear me through the darkness,

Will I make it to you?

Can you hear me, please give me a clue,

Or will I fade to silence in the darkness

of you.

I walk out into the darkness
reaching to the sky. The moon
has cast a glow that blinds my
tearful eye...

I wrap my arms around
it thinking it was you
only to realize it's just the
morning's dew.

The road to home

is long,

my heart is singing

our song.

I hear it and smile,

I've been away for a while.

I hope your still there

and that you really care.

I know I just want you

to be mine,

I swear!

Be yourself,

not what people want you to be.

Change only what you want

them to see.

Ocean Blue

Look deep into the ocean blue

of my eyes

Let the waves of passion

  beat

against unknown places in your mind.

Together we will drown

in the sea of love

until the tides take us away.

Your lips make me feel like I'm dancing on
moonbeams and skipping from star to star,
floating in the night sky to fill your dreams
of loving me from afar.

I want to be a bloom
in your garden of love.
So you can kiss
the sweet dewdrops
and sweet nectar
from my petals.
To embrace my stem
to the roots of my love
and fertilize them
to last forever.

Look up

and watch

the stardust dancing

in the night.

This will make you happy,

That you are in this life.

Twinkle, Twinkle, Little Heart

I want to be the twinkle

in your eyes,

The smile on your face,

The excitement

in your step

but most of all,

the love in every breath

you take.

I want the wind of the sea
to set me free,
the waves and water
splash over me.
To feel the sea air
makes me not care.
I'm lost in my mind
I know no kind.
The water sets my mind
at ease
I don't worry
if I please.
The salt lays heavy on my skin
yet I always go back in.
It cleanses me that way,
that feeling lets me say.
I love this wind,
that my mind is in.

I'm hungry for the garden of love
to be fertilized with the fruits of
passion and fill my heart and soul
to grow with forever love.

Tranquil Quill

I float through my dreams
tranquility and peace it seems.
Even in the dark,
I see,
all the love for you to be.
Never to toss it away
my love for you will stay.
Kiss the darkness of the night
to awaken with you in my sight.
Holding on without fear that
your love will always be here.

Do you feel?

Are they real?

Touch my face.

Any place.

Can you see

the pain in me?

Heartbeat eyes

really cry.

Feel my mind.

Hurt not kind.

Will it be

ever for me?

When I see

you are me.

I look in the mirror of me
and see nothing but the ghosts
of what I used to be.

Rich Like a King

When your young you dream
of being rich like a king.
Thinking about being a doctor or nurse.
A fireman or policeman is your thing.
You dream of love and marriage abound
like in the fairytales it sounds.
Oh, don't forget about the big house,
like Cinderella without the mouse.
Daydream about kids playing ball,
waiting for you to say dinner, you call.
Then when you're older
you look back on those dreams,
realize it was none of those things.
It's all about love and peace of mind,
That's what is so special,
that's what's so kind.
To look back and see
this life is mine, this life is me.

Gone like the wind
never to be again.
When night falls
it's no more.
That feeling is a dream,
not there through it all.
Mornings come and go
never to show.
Feelings of peace,
even sleep,
missing the beat.
Taking my breath,
traveling through
the mind,
lost in time.
Will never be,
loved.

I thought it was just the mornings dew...

...but it was really my
tears from missing you.

We all have invested
our heart and soul into
someone we have banked
on that has emptied our
safe of love.

Til Death Do Us

I want that love that lasts forever

A love that never says never.

Puts my heart at ease

That I want to please.

Til death do us part,

Is said from the heart.

Not just words to say,

Then just leave one day.

A love I can hold,

My heart is told.

Is there really such a thing?

No, too much pain.

There is no til death,

It's always do us part,

And that my dear

Breaks the heart.

Let My Brush *Go...*

I need to motivate me

to paint what I see,

to write poems of truth

regardless of the root.

To make me better so I can feel

and my pen writes so real.

Paint from my heart,

capture every part.

Too busy my brain,

cause it keeps us sane.

Let my brush go.

To where?

Who knows.

My pen flows at night

what my mind fights.

To grow old and stay real—

to continue to feel.

My alone is more
lonesome than lonely.

Sometimes my life is written in
the stars. They remind me of the
twinkling in your eyes that will forever
touch my beating heart until the
darkness has forever engulfed my soul.

From Seed To Leaf

From seed to leaf,

we grow and weep.

Our leaves will blow

when it's time to go.

As the wind takes us away,

we seed for others along our way,

never to die in their minds we stay.

Rest easy when you see,

my leaf blowing in the breeze.

Don't worry I'm still there

Take care of the seed I left

everywhere.

Here Comes The Angels

When angels come to visit,
they're sent by loved ones from afar,
who wants to check on you and
see just how you are.
They always follow the light way.
This is what they choose
their path brings you peace
and sweet dreams you never lose.
Remember when you close your eyes,
your family has been there
brought to you by the angels,
sent to you by your loved ones with care.

We all go through life
on a different path...

only to end up at the
same place.

Paint To Feel

My brush doesn't just paint
what I see,
it paints where one's mind
wants to be.
Not just walking in the sand,
feeling the grains upon the hands.
The wind tasting of salt,
blowing all it can.
Sun shining so bright,
warmth wrapping one so tight.
Close your eyes, be still
imagine what you feel.

It can be the beach

or the woods,

I paint everything I could.

A summers breeze,

given by the trees,

the warmth of the sun

walking becomes fun.

Creatures high and low

playing to and fro.

Close your eyes and see

the wonder in the trees.

I paint not just to be.

I paint what others enjoy to see.

I hope when you throw stones
                    it builds your stairway
                    down
                        to
                            hell.

Come to me, not just at night
Come to me, when it's right.
Come to me, because you care
Come to me, your feelings bare.
Come to me, they'll be no harm
Come to me, wrap in your arms
Come to me, we can play
Come to me, this is our day.

I can see you
on angels wings,
coming to talk to me
about things.
A visit I need
so much this day,
I just want to hear
you say.
I'm watching over you
sending love
your way.
I'm so sorry my visit
will not last,
I love talking
about the past.

I must go, so go back
to sleep,
I'm always there
when your heart beats.
I awaken to see,
were you here
with me,
I found a feather,
on my pillow I see.
You were here,
I feel such peace
I'll save the feather
for all my sleep.

If I could have changed
anything it would have been
your heart.

I wish I could lay next to you

Like years ago when we were new

Lay close just one more time.

Let our lost love entwine.

Hold me to you really tight,

As if it again was our last night.

When I feel you near

Their is peace no fear

The love fills my heart

It could burst apart

As long as your here

Everything is clear

My love for you

Will last for years

Never to die

Or cry to say goodbye.

You will always be apart

Of my living heart

Tossing Words

I toss my words into the darkness and
watch them dance on angels wings
bringing peace to everyone in all of Gods
beautiful things.
Spilling out for all to hear
Making all around them crystal clear.
Whispering words of peace
While all our eyes are closed and sleep.
Waking gently to a brand new day
Thinking about those angels words and
how peaceful is our day.

I want to make you laugh,

And to make you sigh.

I want for you to see me

With love in your eyes.

I want you to hold me

Like you won't let me go.

I want you to love me

And let the world know.

I want you to whisper

I am all you need

I want to be your soil

Where you will plant your seed.

Star light, star bright

Your the only star tonight.

Through the day I know your near.

At night I hold you oh so dear.

My love for you is all day long,

And grows so strong, so very strong.

In the dark or in the light

Your star will always be so bright.

To my first true love,
you know who you are.
Watched you from a distance,
you were always way too far.
I saw you through the years
holding back my tears.
Wondering if you ever thought of me
and how our love use to be.
Now I'm older, knowing you are too,
getting to know you would be new.
I now have no one, just like you,
it's time for us to start over again,
and enjoy each other just as friends.
To maybe become lovers,
until the very end.

Become Two

I want to lay beside you

so we can become two.

Just want you to hold me,

like you use to do.

My first love, you will always be,

you're the one that holds the key,

to again open my heart,

to set my love for you free.

Lay close and whisper in my ear,

this is what you wanted to hear.

BECKY WALLACE

Pandemic Prose

Lies of Our Lives

Are you woke

or have you *WOKE* up?

Fakebook

Welcome to the land of Fakebook,

Where everyone's life is a fairytale.

I scroll, I read and I look.

Some people are open books.

I wonder to myself, is everything so fine

Cause everything ain't fine in mine.

Life is hard and not always

a piece of cake.

Why do so many let on like it's so great?

It looks like we have so many friends

Trust me, ya don't in the end.

Theirs just a few who I really knew.

I was glad to see them too.

Someday you will laugh and see

Facebook was no place to be.

So Called King

Bow down to your so called king,
He lives in the west wing.
His servants make the rules
He just gives them the tools.
They know he's not all there
So they lead him everywhere.
He doesn't remember their names,
To him, it's just a game.
Their moves are like in chess
To destroy and leave a mess.
He can not speak without them,
So they all know they win.
Bow down to their so called king
Just keep him in the wing.
They will make the rules.
Using their new tools.
Be very aware,
we have become the fools!

Vaccine, vaccine, get your vaccine!

They hawk their wares everywhere
I've seen.
Line um up, car after car
It's there, not too far.
Get um while you can,
The cries from the police, for the man.
Get um' while they're hot, in the arm
They will be good said big pharm.
Don't worry about all that's died
Hold that paper up with pride.
That shot won't last long
Sorry they were wrong
Vaccine, vaccine get another vaccine
And vaccine, vaccine, vaccine until.

Listen to the old ones.

They know what's best.

If you don't like something,

Then go show the unrest.

Some old political rich

Want you to fill the niche,

Stand your ground,

Confront who is all around.

If they don't comply,

Auntie will make them cry

She will help you

So don't you sigh

So burn and loot and beat them down

Cause Auntie Max wears the crown.

She will be at your sides

She will watch as you shoot

And watch as they die.

She feels an eye for an eye is why.

Afraid To Be Me

I never thought I would see

a time I didn't feel free.

I'm actually afraid to be me.

I'm scared about the way things are,

they are taking this all way too far.

The roads I want to travel in my car

not allowed to go that far.

Must have a passport they say

to visit my country the USA.

If you don't comply you fail,

you could end up in jail.

Is this how I've dreamed it would be?

Never in my lifetime,

not me.

Mask up for compliance!

Mask down for freedom!

Staring at the sunlight

darkness is what I see.

Why can't others understand?

Can't they read?

They want us all in darkness,

while they hide their evil ways.

if we don't comply,

our darkness will be the caves.

No more sunlight to bring any joy

we will live in darkness as before.

Do you want your freedom,

or become their human toy?

My heart is aching so bad
and feeling so, so sad.
For our nation
we once knew
is gone for me
and you.
Everything has changed
to never be the same.
Capture those memories
and hold them near.
Cause all we know
is lost in fear.

He is among us
I fear, he's real
walking on the
souls of Evil.

Friend or Foe?

Are you resisting the truth
believing their lies?
Are you believing the truth
resisting their lies?
I'm confused as to why
anyone would believe all the lies.
Do you even try to seek what's right?
Or just accept the lies on sight?
Do your homework and you will see,
the lies are meant to fool you and me.
Read history about the way things were,
the lies are told so you con-cur.
They want you to think all is great.
Their lies will show you their hate.
We are nothing to them,
they are not your friend
You must believe they're your enemies til
the bitter end.
Friend or foe?
Foe I know,
now.

The mask,

what did I wear it for?

So I could walk through the door.

I wore it forever, all around,

Now I'm throwing it on the ground.

Wearing it made me seethe,

now I can finally breathe.

No more a mask,

I will wear,

they might say I must,

but I don't care.

Now I can breathe easy every day

With freedom,

that's my way.

They Lie

They lie.
They shout.
Line up.
No doubt.
Don't fear.
You're clear.
  Next.
They cheer.
They lie.
You shout.
You doubt.
You fear.
Not clear.
Fear.

Down To Sleep

Now I lay me down to sleep,
my mind sometimes begins to weep.
I miss the times we lived and played
cause it sure is not that way these days.
My eyes are closed,
full of tears,
nowadays they cry with fear.
Not knowing what may happen
anymore,
Will they come knocking at the door?
They won't be playing around this time,
they're going to take what is mine.
I will fight them to the bitter end,
with all my heart I will defend.
All I love and worked hard for
will not be taken out my door.
Fighting them tooth and nail,
Trust me I won't fail.

Can you people not see

the major tyranny?

They will require a vaccine

for you to even be seen.

A prisoner to them

Are you going to let them win?

Wake up,

get smart ,

we need to start standing for

what's right.

Begin our fight.

Freedom we need

or we all will bleed.

Negativity is just too much

some use this as a crutch.

I scroll each day

and see what you say.

Hurtful things cause

some do not think your way.

Why not be nice to all who see?

Wouldn't you rather be?

I'm tired of hiding what you say

I just can't let you ruin my day.

You must hate being this way.

I hope you change how you feel.

Start seeing what is real.

Be happy what you write,

you will rest easier at night.

I see.

I hear.

I feel.

Sadness.

Lies.

Tears.

Emotional.

Fear.

Pain.

Life.

Gone.

Insane.

Our lives will never be the same,
they are playing a deadly game.
My eyes are tired from seeing
how that things are being.
Life is really hard and sad,
this should make you so mad.
Suppose to accept what we see,
that's not how it's supposed to be.
We all just believe and hide,
instead of fighting this,
side by side.
We need to show our strength,
regardless of what they think.
Band us together,
we will stay strong forever.
Will march for our states,
with love in our hearts,
not HATE!

Here I Am

Here I am,
existing in a country,
   I don't know.
Here I am,
an old person with what purpose,
   I don't know.
Here I am,
scared of what,
   I don't know.
Here I am,
alone with thoughts,
   I don't know.
Here I am
with tears for what,
   I don't know.
Here I am here,
why?
   I don't know.
Here I am, here.

Times are dark, getting darker by the day.

The light we once knew has been snuffed out by the darkness of evil to never be spoken of again. We are dead to them, the evil we are seeing has not a care for us. Power and greed have darkened the way we live, we think, we exist! If you think different be aware they will find you and you will not exist anymore. They locked us down to now locking us up. Prisoners of political war. We need to rise up and break out of this darkness. Until we do our days are numbered to become the darkest of our lives.

Emotional Breaths

Surely one can feel the tightening of the emotional cord being tightened with every breath we take. No longer can one look back and enjoy artistic forms we all cherished from before. Darkened or changed to fit these non emotional times we are being blasted with, literally taken to the dark side. The screen no longer shows us laughter, joy or true heartbreak. Poof only true lies and mass confusion to warp the minds of the weak.

Taking away the gatherings of life's loved ones. Controlling our emotions with the cord of darkness. The art of expressing ones ability to seek the truth is blackened by the screen of lies. One needs to go back in your mind and relive the art of having a life. To sense again the joy of living. Bring that emotion back to now. Only then can you see that ones light is being blackened by the darkness of the way we are told to be.

What terrifies me the most is how brainwashed people like them have become. The biggest threat to our democracy isn't an ex-president (*FYI their guy won*) but it is a culture of thinkless thinkers like them who cannot see beyond the MSNBC, CNN, NY Times, Washington Post headlines. It's the folks like them who beat their chest proudly with propagandized, partisan bullet points as if they're a savant, when in actuality they're just like every other brainwashed zombie, reciting the same talking points.

I Fear

I fear for my mind
and all mankind.
I fear to love again
that it will only end.
I fear anymore
all the way to my core
I fear for the insane
they have become so vain.
I fear for the good
that it's so misunderstood.
I fear my dreams
hear too many screams.
I fear this life
too many strifes.
I fear that light
will become all night
I fear the 'we.'
I fear me.
I fear.

The speech was so bland

saddens me for our land.

Surely you could see

where he wants us to be.

He doesn't know the truth

his mind is too aloof.

I'm sure he wasn't there

he was watching from somewhere.

The Truth he wouldn't know

lies are written on the scroll.

Read on,

nothing he says is true,

he cares not for me and you.

It Is

It is light against dark.

It is us against them.

It is freedom against prison.

It is dreams against nightmares.

It is living against not.

It is life against death.

It is us saving us against their destruction.

It is our constitution against their ways.

It is our rights against power.

It is time to raise up against them.

It is our country.

It is ours.

It is .

I'm awake

Not woke

I hear them

It's a joke

I'm awake

It's free

Woke won't

Get to me.

I'm awake

I see,

Darkness

In front

Of me

I'm awake

I know

What way

To go

I'm awake

not woke

I'm awake

No joke

I'M AWAKE!!!

I'M FREE

TO ME!!!!!

Today Was That Day

Today was that day

you wonder what I'll say?

We were told to lock our doors

don't walk, breathe or play.

Stay off the roads

that's what we were told.

Not allowed to dine or to go get any wine.

Sunday's became not a day of rest,

because you can't worship or pray,

you might be under arrest.

Stay off the roads,

better not drive your car.

only if you must and not very far.

You're not allowed to breathe,

a mask is what you need.

You wear them with care,

make sure it's everywhere.

Their numbers don't lie

or do they, we cry.

Everything we have been through

we were warned,

we might die.

A year we have suffered

for what we cry

So they can get richer

From nothing but lies.

Our freedom, money,

and lives they have taken

Don't you think it's time for us

to be more Awake-End?

What part of freedom is making us wear masks?

What part of freedom is taking this vaccine?

What part of freedom is never seeing family?

What part of freedom is not flying without a mask?

What part of freedom is government telling you what you can and can't do?

What part of freedom is ok for government to take your livelihoods?

What part of freedom don't you understand?

What part of this all is free?

Prisoner's Home

My mind races ahead of me,
I don't like this not being free.
I feel like a prisoner in my own home
sitting here every day all alone,
thinking again how nice it would be to just roam.
Hear laughter and playing from so many of our own,
sitting and eating from this very home.
So sad are the days being alone,
all we can do is call from our phones.
Our phones become life but it doesn't ease the strife.
It makes us miss more how things use to be,
when everyone one of us was very free.
Don't forget about others,
some lost their fathers and mothers.
They have no one to see,
how hard it is to not be free.
Dream on every day from the silence of home,
maybe just maybe we all again can roam.

The longer you mask up
your freedom,
the longer your freedom
is masked!

Normalcy is the joke
that laughs forever.

Become The Light

My mind is so confused,

as the darkness engulfs my head.

I am becoming a shadow

of the darkness

where I'm afraid I've lost my way.

Which I'm not sure if anymore,

which way I need to go.

Do I follow the darkness

as my light fades away?

Can I stop the darkness

to find another day?

I'm so afraid

of the darkened shadows of life

that it will swallow me more

every night.

I pray to see
if even a sliver of light
that my mind can find peace
at night.
Do I become the darkness
of shadows
or do I claw my way
towards that sliver of light?
Will this darkness
ever ease my life?
In some way where the light
will increase my thoughts
so I can climb away?
I can only sleep and pray
that the darkness is shredded
by the light
of another beautiful day.

I hate the hate we see today,

it really just gets in the way.

This hate will not set you free,

our God is in control,

don't you see?

Hate, I'm afraid, is here to stay,

I'm getting afraid to think about

what to say.

Are we ever going to see the end,

where people go back to being friends?

If I take a knee it's to pray to God,

that our country heals from all the fraud.

All these lies and hate are so real,

is this truly how some feel?

I sure hope to see the day,

Where we all join hands,

to make a better way.

I Want

I want to feel the beating of my heart.

I want to feel this as my day starts.

I want to feel the sun on my face.

I want to drive fast like I'm in a race.

I want the wind to mess up my hair.

I want it to blow awry with not a care.

I want to run like a deer.

I want to feel no fear.

I want to feel the dirt between my toes.

I want to play all day and let no one know.

I want to be humble and kind.

I want to be that to all that I find.

I want to feel the darkness of night.

I want it to wrap the stars around me tight.

I want to be free,

I want to be,

I want,

Free.

Put your arm out they say
Take the vaccine,
it's ok.
I promise a cure
if you do it today.
Put your arm out
the problems are few,
it's been tested,
it's all normal and new
Put your arm out,
it's no lie.
Put your arm out
they laugh,
then you start to cry.
Thinking out loud
what if this makes me...
you sigh.

In the coming days you will see
A war among us in this country
The hatred of them towards one man
Because he found out their evil plans.

They were finally able to close his door
Bringing their socialist ways afore
Fencing in the devil on capital hill,
Telling us you no longer have your will.

They are guarded all day
We the people must pay
Don't ever speak your mind
They will silent all of your kind

The power is there's
No care if it's fair
Stay home, sit in the dark
This is your only free park.

Be Still and Listen

Be still and listen to the beat
a heart crying from defeat.
When will people standup for real
and fight for what they steal?

Shout from your heart,
it is time to start.
Fight for what is to be,
take back what belongs to thee

Our country is in jeopardy,
surely you can see.
Start fighting for what is real,
not the lies they want you to feel

The virus is no longer real,
the vaccine will soon be a pill.
No need to worry,
it was a lie told to you in a story.

Read on,
your just a pawn
to their political game
play on.
Soon you will see,
They could care less
about you and me.

With A Stroke Of His Pen

With the stroke of his pen
So many's days came to an end
Millions lost their income
and their lives
With the stroke of his pen
your world took a nosedive.

With the stroke of his pen
all women can no longer win
Women's sports are now for men
who can take what we have earned
Cause they really don't care
if we are burned.

With the stroke of his pen,
let everyone in
They are all free
to take what belongs to me.
He gave them everything for free.

With the stroke of his pen
Over and over again,
All of our lives
Are slowly coming to an end.

With the stroke of his pen
The elite have no sins.
They will wine and dine
On us all as the reset begins

With the stroke of his pen,
We are nothing to him
With the stroke of his pen
Our freedom will end.

With the stroke of his pen.

Yes,
Most of Us Voted

Yes most of us voted
but some were not noted.
Some became the winners
cause you choose a sinner.

His first day he was there,
he signed away without care.
I hope now you see
how awful things will be.

Sign away, sign away that's what he did,
sitting there acting like a big kid.
Laughing at all of you that voted him in,
oh, hide your guns behind the gin.

Yes you get what you sow,
I hope now you know,
he's not there for you
they won the big coup.

Be careful what you wish for,
it will knock at your door.
He will take away all,
so you will be poor.

The division in our

country is real

Only because of

their steal.

You can say it's not true,

you need to educate,

the you.

Read the facts,

instead of believing

the *whacks*,

You will be shocked,

and your world will be rocked,

Take the time to see

what they tell you will be

You need to listen

or our world can not be free.

I'm so upset about what I've seen,
I really wonder what it all means.
Are we truly ever going to be free,
I'm afraid it looks not to be.

I'm so upset about what I've seen,
now I know exactly what it means.
The rich can go through ever for,
and they will always have more.

All you others, you will see,
There's nothing left for thee.
They will rule you to the ground,
You will become the rabbit
for the hounds.

They will make sure you never see,
The light of day trust me
You aren't free.
They will take it all
You will have to bow down to them
in their hall.

Oh Say, Do You See?

Is it just me or does anyone else feel like they are not free? Do you smother behind your mask? Do you dream of another time, when you did everything and more, never thinking about doing nothing all the time and being bored?

Remember when you saw your loved ones whenever you wanted, regardless of if they were home one in the hospital, or wherever. Do you think about going out to dinner with your better half, just because? Going to see school plays or ballgames so you get to brag about your kids? Teacher's meetings to see how they are doing or having birthday parties with all their friends. Vacations with family and friends?

Just living your life? Believing what they say on the news cause you knew it was true? You had your dream job, remember?

People you need to wake up, these things and many more have been taken from most of us. This is wrong. We are the people of this United States of America. WE ARE NOT CHINA OR ANY OTHER COMMUNIST RULE COUNTRY. We need to take back our lives and make those who want to destroy us be held accountable. If you cant see this is happening then you are not listening. Hear us now, this is happening and only we can free ourselves! Quit making decisions with your emotions and educated yourself. Take back what is rightfully ours.

What is wrong with people today?

What is wrong with people today?
Why do some act this way?
I know we all do not agree,
but why, I just can't see.

Some things people say
to others every day,
does this make them
feel good in some way?

I wonder how they can sleep at night,
when all they do is keep up a fight.
I wonder if they ever feel bad,
for what they say is so sad.

Social Media was not supposed
to be,
where people fought about
what's free.

We are all free to say
what we please,
we all have opinions you know,
but this is how people grow.

I'm saddened as can be
to live in this country,
to be so divided
we will never see unity.

Because some people won't stop
what they say,
so this America can heal
today.

Living In The Now

We all should be living in the now
some have lost just 'how.'
Learn just how to play,
to make it through the day.

Things have been hard for a while,
some have forgotten how to smile.
Worrying whose side they're on,
when we are all truly just their pawns.

Think twice about words you say,
you may hurt some,
then you will pay.
Our written words won't go away,
because of the times,
they are here to stay.

Speak only words from your heart,
be true with the words of your part.
Our words should not bring others
to tears,
they should make you smile from
ear to ear.

Stay kind in your loving way,
learn again just how to play.
Think of all the ones you made smile,
You gave them that,
which will last a long while.

The Positive,
Spin

We need to put a positive spin
on life today,
we need to learn just how to play.
We should always think about
what we say,
it may help or hurt someone that day.

Things are different
than what we once knew,
we look at things deeper,
through and through.
What we say can hurt someone
and we really think that's fun?

Open your heart and eyes, these things
we say, can't you hear the cries?
We are all God's children, can't you see?
We all deserve to be free.

We all should be able to say the pledge
and this act not cause a wedge.
We are all different now
so bow your head and pray,
We all should want to see a better day.

It changes life when the hub of a family leaves you, gone are traditions, gone in your heart. When they're gone you lose the sounds of joy, holidays become only half noisy and they never have the warm feeling of home. Now we are all losing another hub, our country, our freedom our voice. We will never view our lives the same way. We have lost our hub. The only difference is we might get it back but we will never treat it the same. No more will we take it for granted, abuse it or forget it. Our minds will think differently and be more aware of what's taking place. She belongs to us not them. Only we the people can get her back. We must fight and pray that our efforts are for not! We must take our home back, our hub, and make it great again. We the people of the United States of America!

We are the old that have been used the young ones think that's our dues. We have lived in the better days where no one was made to feel their age but we have lived to watch them turn the page of years of history we went through with no thoughts of the fact we made. We cared for old and young with respect for what they had done. Today some want our lives to disappear and change us where we will fear.

We must make others see that we represent our history and made this land what they see. We won't change to fit their way, they too should have to pay. Freedom cost from years gone by. You suffer with tears when they cry. Be gone this beautiful land that be, they don't care if we are free. They want our land that was built by hand and all we have for power and greed. We must fight again so they won't be. We must fight for this land so we will remain free!

I want to thank everyone who has been in my life, left my life, has hung in there with me through my life, and are in my life, now.

Thank you.

BECKY WALLACE

Oldisms, Poetry
& Pandemic Prose

Becky J. Wallace

etsy.com/shop/beckyjwallaceart